Every

SON

should have
a book
like this...

Other Titles in This Series:

*Every Daughter Should Have a Book like This
to Remind Her How Wonderful She Is*

*Every Mom Should Have a Book like This
Filled with Love and Appreciation*

*Every Sister Should Have a Book like This
to Let Her Know What a Blessing She Is*

All writings are by Douglas Pagels except as noted.

Library of Congress Control Number: 2007907773
ISBN: 978-1-59842-311-2

M and Blue Mountain Press are registered in U.S. Patent and Trademark Office. Certain trademarks are used under license.

Acknowledgments appear on page 72.

Printed in China.
First Printing: 2008

 This book is printed on recycled paper.

This book is printed on fine quality, laid embossed, 80 lb. paper. This paper has been specially produced to be acid free (neutral pH) and contains no groundwood or unbleached pulp. It conforms with the requirements of the American National Standards Institute, Inc., so as to ensure that this book will last and be enjoyed by future generations.

Blue Mountain Arts, Inc.
P.O. Box 4549, Boulder, Colorado 80306

Every

SON

*should have
a book
like this*

*filled with wishes,
love, and
encouragement*

Douglas Pagels

Blue Mountain Press™
Boulder, Colorado

Contents

Remember What Reba Said...

{My son is} the greatest thing that has ever happened to me! He is the absolute highlight of my life.

He is my sunshine. He is... what unconditional love is all about.

— Reba McEntire

Thank You for Being the Wonderful Son That You Are

I wish I could find the words to tell you how great it is to be the parent of a son like you.

The perfect words would tell you how proud I am of all you've done and everything you've become...

The ideal words would say what a joy it was to watch you grow up, and what an amazing and rewarding and loving experience it continues to be.

Every time I see you, I know that I am looking at as treasured a gift as anyone has ever been given.

And I know that I could have hoped and prayed and dreamed all my life... and I could have wished on a million stars...

But I couldn't have been blessed with anyone more wonderful... than the son that you are.

Remember What Kenny Said...

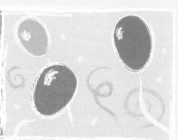

When [the midwife] announced, "It's a beautiful baby... boy," cheers went up from the team. Ten seconds later it hit me. Boy?! Baby boy! My joy mixed with confusion. I was so sure it was going to be a girl, I hadn't even considered the possibility of a boy. I quickly recovered a little of my composure as [she] handed him to me.

It took me all of ten seconds to bond to this new little guy for the rest of my life.

— Kenny Loggins

Son, when you came into this world and into my life, so many extraordinary things happened. Although I was the one holding you, you were the one enfolding so many of my hopes and dreams. Although I was the one who was supposed to teach you all the things to do as you grew up, you were the one who taught me — constantly — of my capacity to love, to experience life in its most meaningful way, and to open my heart wide enough to let all those feelings inside.

Everywhere you journey in life, you will go with my love by your side.

Forever it will be with you. Truly, joyfully, and more meant to be than words could ever say. You are the joy of my life, the source of my dearest memories, the inspiration for my fondest wishes, and you are the sweetest present life could ever give to anyone.

Remember What Linda Said...

I am unutterably proud of my son and happy to do whatever I can to make sure the rest of the world feels the same way.

— Linda Armstrong Kelly

You're not just a fantastic son. You're a tremendous, rare, and extraordinary person. All the different facets of your life — the ones you reveal to the rest of the world and the ones known only to those you're close to — are so impressive. And as people look even deeper, I know they can't help but see how wonderful you are inside.

I'll always love you, Son, with all my heart. And I couldn't be more proud of you... if I tried.

Has anyone told you lately what a wonderful person you are?

I hope so! I hope you've been told dozens of times... because you are just amazing.

And just in case you haven't heard those words in a while, I want you to hear them now. You deserve to know that...

It takes someone special to do what you do. It takes someone rare and remarkable to make the lives of everyone around them nicer, brighter, and more beautiful. It takes someone who has a big heart and a caring soul. It takes someone who's living proof of how precious a person can be.

It takes someone... just like you.

Son, right before my eyes, you have grown up so much on your way to becoming the special person you are today.

From a baby, to a boy, to a young man, you were full of life and filled with surprises. Trying to keep up with you has been many things: rewarding, challenging, hopeful, and fulfilling. In every one of your years, you have given me more happiness and love than most people will ever dream of.

Remember What Peter Said...

And of course it's my kids, way more than anything else, that remind me every minute how incredibly lucky I have been on this earth.

My children know I love them. If I'm sure of anything, I'm sure of that. But I wonder if they realize that even the smallest details of their lives have been unspeakably precious to me.

— Peter Barton

Sometimes we need reminders in our lives of how much people care. If you ever get that feeling, I want you to remember this...

I love you, Son. Beyond words that can even begin to tell you how much...

I hold you and your happiness within my heart each and every day. I am so proud of you and so thankful to the years that have given me so much to be thankful for.

If I were given the chance to be anything I wanted to become, there's nothing I would rather be than your parent.

And there is no one I would rather have... as my son.

Remember What
Paul Said...

One day shortly after my son's birth, I found myself remaining in my office... gazing at one of the eleven hundred pictures of my boy I had surrounded myself with, and just marveling.

— Paul Reiser

I love looking at photographs of you through the years. There are so many great ones! Each one tells a story, and every picture has the ability to take me back in time... clicking the shutter on the first day of school, the big game, this vacation, and that holiday season. There are Halloween costumes, goofy grins, great accomplishments, and just you... being wonderful, amazing you. You're the one with the smiles that will always shine in those pictures.

And I'm the one with the smiles that will stay... forever in my heart.

This Is the Kind
of Son You Are

You're the best kind of son there could ever be. You're the kind who brings so much joy to my heart and who inspires so much gratitude. You're the kind of son whose life is filled with so many possibilities, who receives the happiest hopes, and who needs to know how much he's thought of every single day.

You're the kind of son every parent hopes to have, and I want you to have this... to help you remember that, if I could, I would give you the moon and the sun in return for all the smiles and precious memories you've given me.

In the Course of His Life, a Son Is All These Things

...A little one who is wished wondrous love; a child who is wished endless joy; a boy who is wished understanding and ever-widening circles of knowledge and friendship.

...A teenager who is wished strength in any surroundings, courage in every circumstance, and a recognition of the wonders that await his tomorrows.

...A young man, with paths to walk, bridges to cross, and mountains to climb; and an adult, who may have a child of his own one day... and an opportunity to discover why the love in a parent's heart shines so brightly and in so many ways.

Remember What Kent Said...

Until you have a son of your own, you will never know... the joy beyond joy, the love beyond feeling that resonates in the heart.

— Kent Nerburn

Days Turn into Months, Months Turn into Years

I don't know how it happened, but somehow you grew up. Just. Like. That. I know, and my common sense tells me... that it was a steady progression of seasons going by. But where does the time go? These days, we're so far away from our early beginnings, but happily, wonderfully, and most importantly, we're still so close in our hearts.

As I think back to the days gone by, one of the things I am most grateful for is that you and I never let the days simply slip away. We always tried to make the most of our time together, and I wouldn't trade the memories we made for all the gold at the end of every rainbow.

Nothing was more fun or more fantastic than introducing you to the world and watching the story of your life unfold. We went adventuring, even if it was just in our neighborhood. I loved listening to every question and comment. There were so many absolute gems... and wise words from your fascinating mind even then. Your imagination liked to soar, and so did you.

I remember pushing you in the swing and watching you reach for the sun and the moon and every star in the sky. Together we got lost in so many books, and we found ourselves laughing our heads off at our favorite movies.

Remember What Reeve Said...

As he gets out of the car, Ben is suddenly older, swinging one strap of his backpack over his shoulder.... He needs to leave me now and get into his school self and his classroom, but I can't quite let him go.

"Ben, I have just one thing to say to you. Do you know what it is?"

That I love you deeply....

He smiles. He knows.

— Reeve Lindberg

We ran outside to capture sunsets before they slipped away, and we strolled back in to share dinners and talks and the most precious times my world had ever known. We turned our home into a place where love was and will always be... a constant part of every day.

As time passed so quickly, and as you grew, I remember how you couldn't wait to show me the project or the picture of the day as soon as I'd see you after school. Even though your backpack was almost as big as you were, you never had any problem carrying all your things — and all my dreams for you — on those strong shoulders of yours...

I remember thinking at least a million times what a joy you are to me, and wondering how anyone could love someone as much as I love you.

That precious feeling remains with me right up to this very day. I am simply amazed at how the seasons have flown by, and at how you have grown up so quickly... right before my eyes.

When I look at you, I see someone
I cherish. I see someone I love with
every smile, every hope, every prayer,
and every treasured memory within
me. When I look at you, I see someone
who has so many paths yet to walk,
opportunities to explore, and stars to
keep on reaching for.

As the years go by, my hopes will
travel beside you on all your journeys.
My heart will still be wishing you the
very best, and you will be a joy to
me... all your life.

In your life, which is so precious to me, may troubles, worries, and problems never linger; may they only make you that much stronger and able and wise.

And may you rise each day... with sunlight in your heart, success in your path, answers to your prayers, and that smile — that I love to see — always there in your eyes.

Remember What Charmian Said...

Someone once told me that children are like kites. You struggle just to get them in the air; they crash; you add a longer tail. Then they get caught in a tree; you climb up and bring them down, and untangle the string; you run to get them aloft again. Finally, the kite is airborne, and it flies higher and higher, as you let out more string, until it's so high in the sky, it looks like a bird. And if the string snaps, and you've done your job right, the kite will continue to soar in the wind, all by itself.

— Charmian Carr

I can barely begin to tell you of all my wishes for you. There are so many of them, and I want them all to come true. I want you to use your heart as a compass as you grow and find your way in the world, but I want you to always have an appreciation for the direction of home. I want you to be self-reliant, self-motivated, and self-sufficient, but also to know that you will never be alone.

If you ever need someone who is just a glance or a word or a phone call away, someone with whom you can share everything that's on your mind — or simply talk about the day, you can always turn to me.

If you ever have a time when you need some encouragement, someone to believe in you, someone to pat you on the back when things have gone right — or to listen to your concerns when they haven't, I will be there for you.

Remember What Matt Said...

...**W**ith my children I think the one thing I want them to remember about me is that no matter what, they can count on me.

— Matt Lauer

If you ever need to know that someone is on the sidelines cheering for you, someone who thinks that you have so much going for you...

Or if you ever need someone to hold the ladder that reaches to your dreams and that climbs to your stars, someone who will never stop appreciating you for being as special as you are...
you can always count on me.

For All the Days to Come

I want your life to be such a wonderful one. I wish you peace. Deep within your soul. Joyfulness. In the promise of each new day. Stars. To reach for. Dreams. To come true. Memories. More beautiful than words can say.

I wish you friends. Close at heart, even over the miles. Loved ones. The best treasures we're blessed with.

Present moments. To live in, one day at a time. Serenity. With its wisdom. Courage. With its strength. New beginnings. To give life a chance to really shine.

I wish you understanding. Of how special you really are. A journey. Safe from the storms and warmed by the sun. A path. To wonderful things. An invitation. To the abundance life brings. And a smile in your heart. For all the days to come.

Something to Light the Way

There are so many new horizons ahead. In the blink of an eye, sons are out the door, off to college, off to jobs, and eventually on to setting up their own homes and tending to their families and future lives. It's a time when parents hope and pray that all the values and lessons they tried to instill will help to light the way for the journey ahead.

Remember What Marian Said...

When my youngest son reached his twenty-first birthday, I began jotting down more lessons to share with him and his two brothers in a world that is ever more challenging. Like most young adults, they do not always welcome or follow parental lessons. But like most mothers, I keep sharing them anyway as lanterns of love I hope will lighten and enlighten their paths....

— Marian Wright Edelman

And I am no exception: I want great things for you, too... and I have an enormous amount of faith in your ability to make your life a happy one. You take with you, everywhere you go, a supply of confidence, common sense, ability, determination, understanding, wisdom, and so many attributes that just sparkle inside you. You know how to make the right choices, and I know that you will.

*But of all the things you take with you,
you should know that you also leave
something behind. Some people call it
an "empty nest," but in its own special
way, there's nothing empty about it. It
will always be abundantly filled with
wishes, support, hugs and hopes, an
open line of communication, a close
and caring bond, a sense of belonging,
and a strong and constant love.*

Remember What Tiger & Earl Said...

As you'll see, my dad is a firm believer that dreams can come true, and I'm living proof that he's right.

— Tiger Woods

Challenge yourself. Dare to stand out from the crowd, to set an example for others, to lead, to shine. You have powers that you haven't even discovered yet, deep inside you, waiting for you to release them. Let them out. Use them to make a difference in your life and in the lives of others. Use your power to care about others; to make solid, responsible choices; and to stand up for what you believe. Dare yourself to set goals that only you can achieve. You are a miracle and you can make miracles happen. Celebrate yourself, love yourself, for all the things that make you special and unique. You are beautiful and wonderful, and I love you.

— Earl Woods

*Through the years, I want you to do
something for me: I want you to go
out of your way to stay healthy in
body and soul. I want you to take
wonderful care of yourself. It goes
along with making good choices and
simply doing things that pay enormous
dividends. Staying healthy and being
wise will benefit every aspect of
your life.*

I want you to have the tools you need to deal with the stress of living in what is sometimes a difficult world. May you never lose your ability to see your way through to the other side of any worries. I hope you'll have enough rainbows in your days to keep you looking up, and enough smiles in your heart to see you through anything.

Son, may you meet every challenge you are faced with, recognize every precious opportunity, and be blessed with the knowledge that you have the ability to make every day special.

May you be strong enough to keep your hopes and dreams alive. May you always be gentle enough to understand. May you have enough material wealth to meet your needs, while never forgetting that the real treasures of life are the loved ones and friends who are invaluable to the end.

Remember What Tom Said...

I *think you can find pleasure in your work, but the things that are truly joyful, joy-producing, well, these are all about your family and friends.*

— Tom Hanks

Twelve Ways to
Keep Smiling

Hold on to your dreams, and never let them go. Show the rest of the world what so many people already know: how wonderful you are!

Give circumstances a chance, and give others the benefit of the doubt. Wish on a star that shines in your sky. Take on your problems one by one and work things out.

Rely on all the strength you have inside. Let loose of the sparkle and spirit that you sometimes try to hide. Stay in touch with those who touch your life with love...

Look on the bright side and don't let adversity keep you from winning. Be yourself, because you are filled with special qualities that have brought you this far and that will always see you through.

Keep your spirits up. Make your heart happy, and let it reflect on everything you do!

Remember What Delores Said...

More than anything, we tried to stress to Michael to enjoy what he was doing. Have a passion for what you are doing and work hard.... If you have a passion, then you are going to be challenged every day to give your best....

Even though sometimes he didn't understand what we were saying, we wanted him to know that what we were teaching him was designed to make him strong once he left our door.

— Delores Jordan

Your Life Story Is Written by You... Day by Day

Each new day is a blank page in the diary of your life. Every day you're given a chance to determine what the words will say and how the story will unfold.

If you work it right, the story of your life will be a wonderful one. The more rewarding you can make each page, the more exquisite the entire book will be. And I would love for you to write a masterpiece...

I want you to have pages on understanding and tales of overcoming hardship. I want you to fill your story with romance, adventure, success, and laughter. I want each chapter to reflect the gift that you are. As you go about your day, I want you to remember...

Goodness will be rewarded. Smiles will pay you back. Have fun. Find strength. Be truthful. Have faith. Don't focus on anything you lack.

Remember that people are the treasures in life and happiness is the real wealth. Have a diary that describes how you are doing your best, and...

The rest will take care of itself.

I know that the best things in life don't come with price tags attached to them. Life's most priceless things are people and families and the love that holds them all together.

How can I ever begin to tell you all the feelings that are inside me and of all the love that is there because of you? There are things I could tell you every day and still not say often enough.

But I want you to always remember that forever and ever I will have a smile inside of me that belongs to you.

Remember What Archie Said...

We are friends. All the football accomplishments, they're all well documented. But what's most important to me — the best times in my life — they've been right in there, in that kitchen, over meals. What's really more important than that?

— Archie Manning
(father of three sons: Peyton, Cooper, and Eli)

A Family Is Love

Wherever we go, and whatever we do, let us live with this remembrance in our hearts... that we are family.

What we give to one another comes full circle. May we always be the best of friends. May we always let our love shine. May we never take for granted what a blessing it is to spend time together.

May we always be one another's rainbow on a cloudy day; as we have been yesterday and today to each other, may we be so blessed in all our tomorrows... over and over again.

For we are a family, and that means love that has no end.

We shared thoughts and hesitations and hopes over morning coffee and afternoon tea. We shared laughter and memories over word games and board games and practical jokes. We shared hugs and tears and respect and appreciation for life and for each other in so many moments....

I will "always remember to play after every storm" because of my hero: my son, and my best friend in the world.

— Jeni Stepanek

There are gifts that are far above priceless. There are memories that are made of pure love. There are special miracles that really do come true.

And all my life, you will always be... a wonderful gift, a treasure of memories, and an amazing miracle... to me.

I don't know if I could ever completely describe to you how important you are to me.

Sometimes you feel like a gift that was given to my days to make sure that they would always have an abundance of happiness in them. More than once I have felt that what I lack in life, I make up for by having a family and a treasure chest of memories that I wouldn't trade for anything. Anytime. Anywhere.

I have dreams in my life that may never come true, travels I may never take, goals I may not be able to reach, and hopes that might always be just beyond my horizons. But I want you to know that whether my wishes come true or whether they disappear altogether, I will always feel like one of the luckiest people in the world.

Because I have such a wonderful son — in you. And I'm going to love you and be proud of you — forever.

I'll always want what is best for you.

I'll try to give you roots, but I'll try to give you wings, too. I want you to feel confident enough to go in the directions you choose, but with the knowledge that wherever you go, you always have a place called home to return to and someone who loves and believes in you.

Remember What Daniel Said...

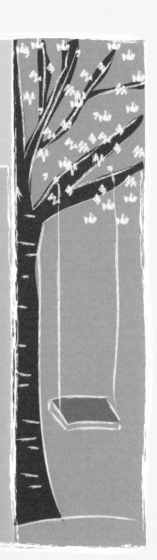

Be thankful that there are people to whom you belong, who love you... who can't think of what they are or what life is without thinking of you.

— *Daniel Taylor*

And now, right as this book is coming to a close, I'm suddenly left wondering... have I said everything that I wanted to say?

Have I expressed each and every hope I have for you? Have I reminded you of all the words of guidance that I want you to use as you find your way in the world? Especially the ones about making good decisions... the kind that will come back to bless you, over and over again?

Have I mentioned that I not only love you as a son, but I like you so much and I admire you as a person?

Have I found a way to say that you have made me as proud as any parent could ever be, and that I can't wait to see what new wonders the years have in store for you?

Have I told you how sincerely I believe that — because you are who you are — because you have a such good heart, such a creative mind, and such an ability to always see your way through — that you will receive all the success and happiness you deserve? And do you know that it couldn't happen to a nicer guy?

And Remember What I Said...

Thank you, Son, beyond all words and for all time for making sure that some of the sweetest memories anyone could ever have ...turned out to be mine.

— *Douglas Pagels*

I hope you know all the things I've tried to say in these pages, along with everything else my heart and I have tried to tell you through the years.

Every time you see this book in the days to come, I hope you'll never forget what an honor it has been... for me to have a son like you. Thank you for enriching my life so much and for being such a blessing to my days. This world would be a far less fascinating, rewarding, and interesting place without you! I'm so glad you're here. I love you a lot...

And I'm more grateful for you than my words can even begin to say.

ACKNOWLEDGMENTS

We gratefully acknowledge the permission granted by the following authors, publishers, and authors' representatives to reprint poems or excerpts from their publications.

Bantam Books, a division of Random House, Inc., for "[My son is…] the greatest thing that has ever…" from COMFORT FROM A COUNTRY QUILT by Reba McEntire. Copyright © 1999 by Reba McEntire. All rights reserved.

HarperCollins Publishers for "When [the midwife] announced…." from THE UNIMAGINABLE LIFE by Kenny and Julia Loggins. Copyright © 1997 by Kenny and Julia Loggins. All rights reserved. And for "One day shortly after my son's birth…" from BABYHOOD by Paul Reiser. Copyright © 1997 by Paul Reiser. All rights reserved.

Broadway Books, a division of Random House, Inc., for "I am unutterably proud of my son…" from NO MOUNTAIN HIGH ENOUGH by Linda Armstrong Kelly. Copyright © 2005 by Linda Armstrong Kelly. All rights reserved.

Rodale, Inc., Emmaus, PA 19098, www.rodalestore.com, for "It's my kids, way more than…" from NOT FADE AWAY: A SHORT LIFE WELL LIVED by Laurence Shames and Peter Barton. Copyright © 2003 by Laurence Shames and Peter Barton. All rights reserved.

New World Library, Novato, CA, www.newworldlibary.com, for "Until you have a son…" from LETTERS TO MY SON by Kent Nerburn. Copyright © 1994, 1999 by Kent Nerburn. All rights reserved.

Simon & Schuster Adult Publishing Group for "As he gets out of the car…" from NO MORE WORDS by Reeve Lindberg. Copyright © 2001 by Reeve Lindbergh. All rights reserved. And for "As you'll see, my dad is a firm believer…" by Tiger Woods and "Challenge yourself" by Earl Woods from START SOMETHING: YOU CAN MAKE A DIFFERENCE by Earl Woods and Tiger Woods Foundation with Shari Lesser Wenk. Copyright © 2000 by Tiger Woods Foundation. All rights reserved. And for "More than anything, we tried…" by Delores Jordan from DRIVEN FROM WITHIN by Michael Jordan. Text copyright © 2005 by Michael Jordan. Compilation copyright © by Rare Air, Inc. All rights reserved.

Penguin Group (USA), Inc., for "Someone once told me that children…" from FOREVER LIESL: A MEMOIR OF THE SOUND OF MUSIC by Charmian Carr. Copyright © 2000 by Charmian Carr and Jean A. S. Strauss. All rights reserved.

Hyperion for "…With my children I think…" by Matt Lauer from BIG SHOES by Al Roker & Friends. Copyright © 2005 by Al Roker. Reprinted by permission of Hyperion. All rights reserved.

Beacon Press for "When my youngest son reached…" from LANTERNS: A MEMOIR OF MENTORS by Marian Wright Edelman. Copyright © 1999 by Marian Wright Edelman. All rights reserved.

Meredith Corporation for "I think you can find pleasure…" by Tom Hanks from "Why We Love Tom Hanks" by Molly Haskell (*Ladies' Home Journal*: April 2001). Copyright © 2001 by Molly Haskell. All rights reserved.

Running Press, a member of Perseus Book Group, for "We are friends" by Archie Manning from FATHERS AND SONS by Todd Richissin. Copyright © 2000 by Todd Richissin. All rights reserved.

Free Press, a division of Simon & Schuster Adult Publishing Group, for "We shared thoughts and hesitations…" by Jeni Stepanek from MY HERO, edited by The My Hero Project. Copyright © 2005 by The My Hero Project. All rights reserved.

Daniel Taylor for "Be thankful that there are people…" from LETTERS TO MY CHILDREN. Copyright © 1989 by Daniel Taylor. All rights reserved.

A careful effort has been made to trace the ownership of selections used in this anthology in order to obtain permission to reprint copyrighted material and give proper credit to the copyright owners. If any error or omission has occurred, it is completely inadvertent, and we would like to make corrections in future editions provided that written notification is made to the publisher:

BLUE MOUNTAIN ARTS, INC., P.O. Box 4549, Boulder, Colorado 80306